I AM OSAGE

How Clarence Tinker Became the First
Native American Major General

By KIM ROGERS   Illustrated by BOBBY VON MARTIN

Heartdrum
An Imprint of HarperCollinsPublishers

Every June since 1942, a big ol' Osage
drum beats in Pawhuska under the hot-as-blue-blazes Oklahoma sun.

BRUM–BUM–BRUM–BUM . . .

And in the dance circle, everyone stands for only one song.

HEY–YAH–HEY–YO . . .

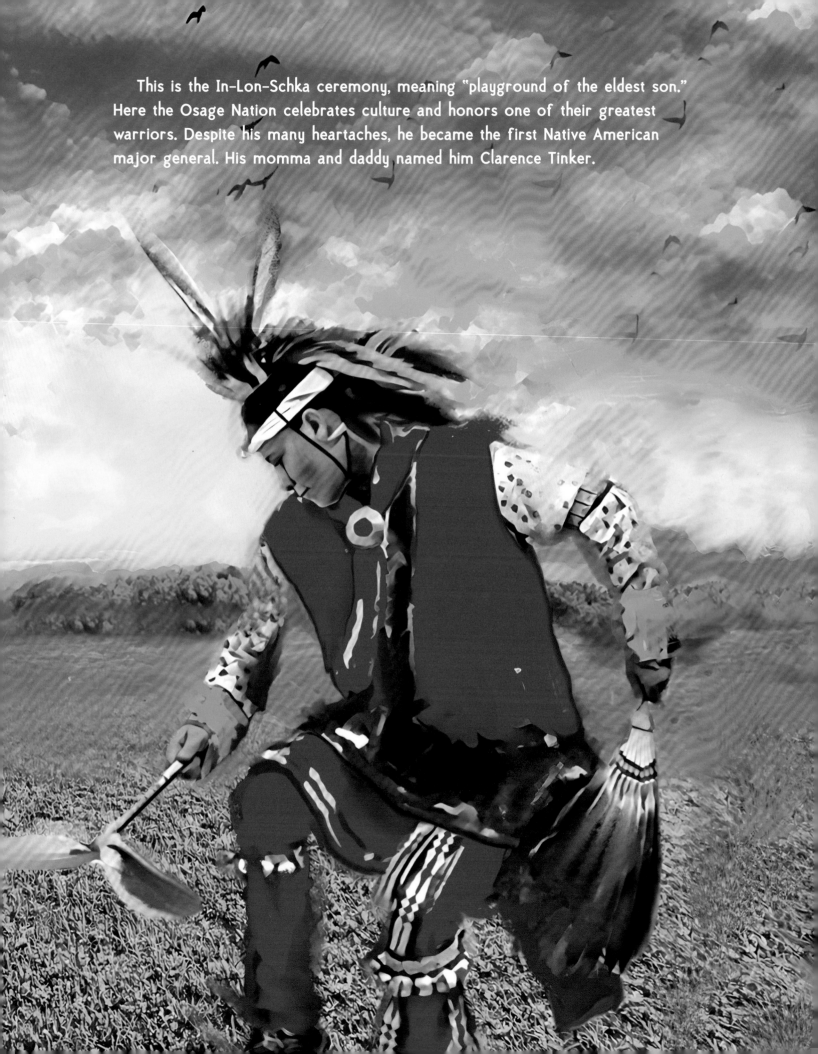

This is the In-Lon-Schka ceremony, meaning "playground of the eldest son." Here the Osage Nation celebrates culture and honors one of their greatest warriors. Despite his many heartaches, he became the first Native American major general. His momma and daddy named him Clarence Tinker.

Clarence was born in the swaying tallgrass prairie of Osage Nation, in Elgin, Kansas, on November 21, 1887.

His folks taught him to respect his Osage heritage and the way his people loved others, even their enemies. They believed in duty, order, commitment, and the teachings of Wahkontah, their Creator.

Clarence hoped to make a difference in the world. He wanted to do something extraordinary. Something adventurous. Something few had ever done before.
But what?
He dreamed.
And dreamed.

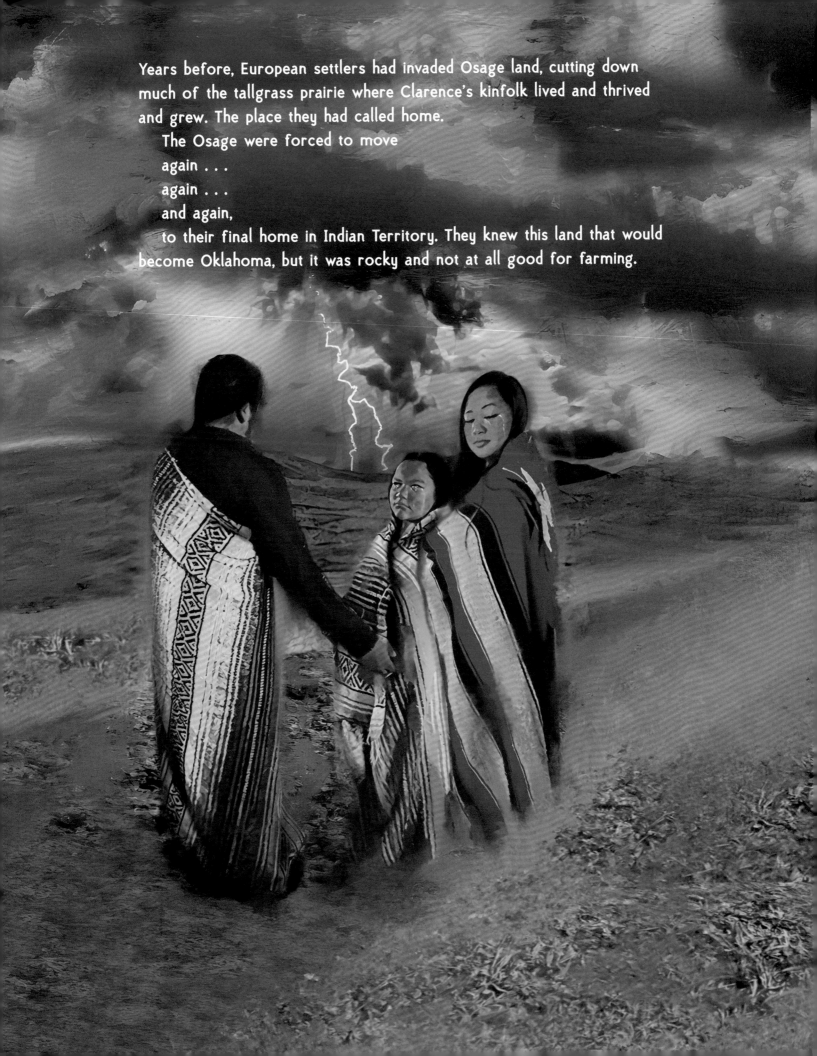

Years before, European settlers had invaded Osage land, cutting down much of the tallgrass prairie where Clarence's kinfolk lived and thrived and grew. The place they had called home.
The Osage were forced to move
again . . .
again . . .
and again,
to their final home in Indian Territory. They knew this land that would become Oklahoma, but it was rocky and not at all good for farming.

The Elders made the difficult decision to give up much of their ways. The Osages were forced to send their children to Indian boarding schools. They feared they would be moved again or worse if they did not do what they were told.

Catholic and Protestant missionaries worked in these schools. They wanted to teach Osage children European ways, even how to follow their God. All because they believed they were better. But that wasn't true at all. Nope.

Clarence said goodbye to his family with hugs and tears and sighs. And he was taken away from them.

The boarding school felt like a prison. Boys and girls were separated. Native kids slept side by side in cold, dark rooms without the warm glow of their families.

Cruel rules.

You must wear clothes *only* like ours.

Harsh tones.

You must speak *only* English!

Heartbreak.

Forget *all* your Osage ways.

But Clarence would never forget.
When he studied his lessons,
or planted seeds,
or chopped wood,
he remembered who and where he came from.
And he would think in Osage and dream in it, too.
No one could take that away from him. No one.

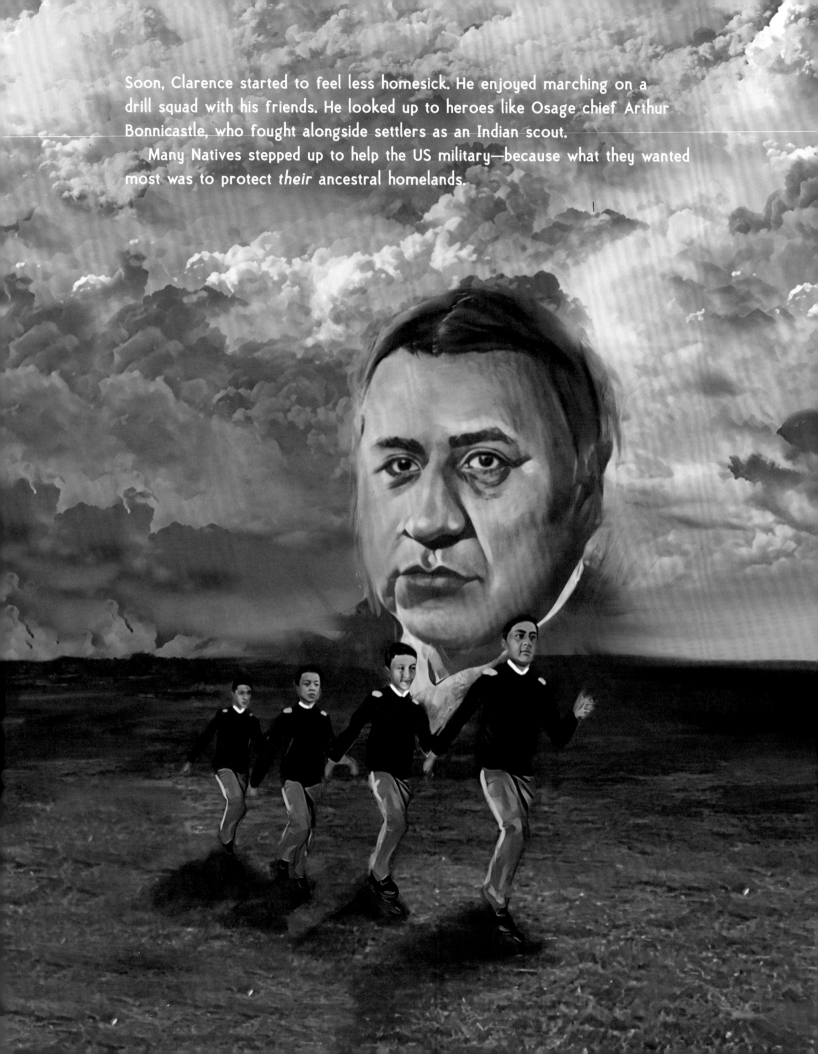

Soon, Clarence started to feel less homesick. He enjoyed marching on a drill squad with his friends. He looked up to heroes like Osage chief Arthur Bonnicastle, who fought alongside settlers as an Indian scout.

Many Natives stepped up to help the US military—because what they wanted most was to protect *their* ancestral homelands.

Clarence was inspired by their commitment to duty. He found the strength to lay down his hurt. Hard as it was, Clarence felt that he had to accept the European way of life.

In high school, Clarence went to Haskell Institute for Indians in Kansas, where he ran track and played on the junior varsity football team. But things weren't easy there, either. More cruel rules. More heartbreak.

So he ran away, back home to the kinfolk he loved.

After a while, he realized that it was important to get an education. But he didn't want to return to his old school. *No, sir.*

A few of his Osage friends got him to enroll in their school, Wentworth Military Academy in Missouri. Pushing pain aside, Clarence did just that.

As he marched to and from class, he thought of being more than an Indian scout. Clarence wanted to serve in the US Army. He wanted to become an officer.

Would they let him in?

I am Osage.

I am Osage.

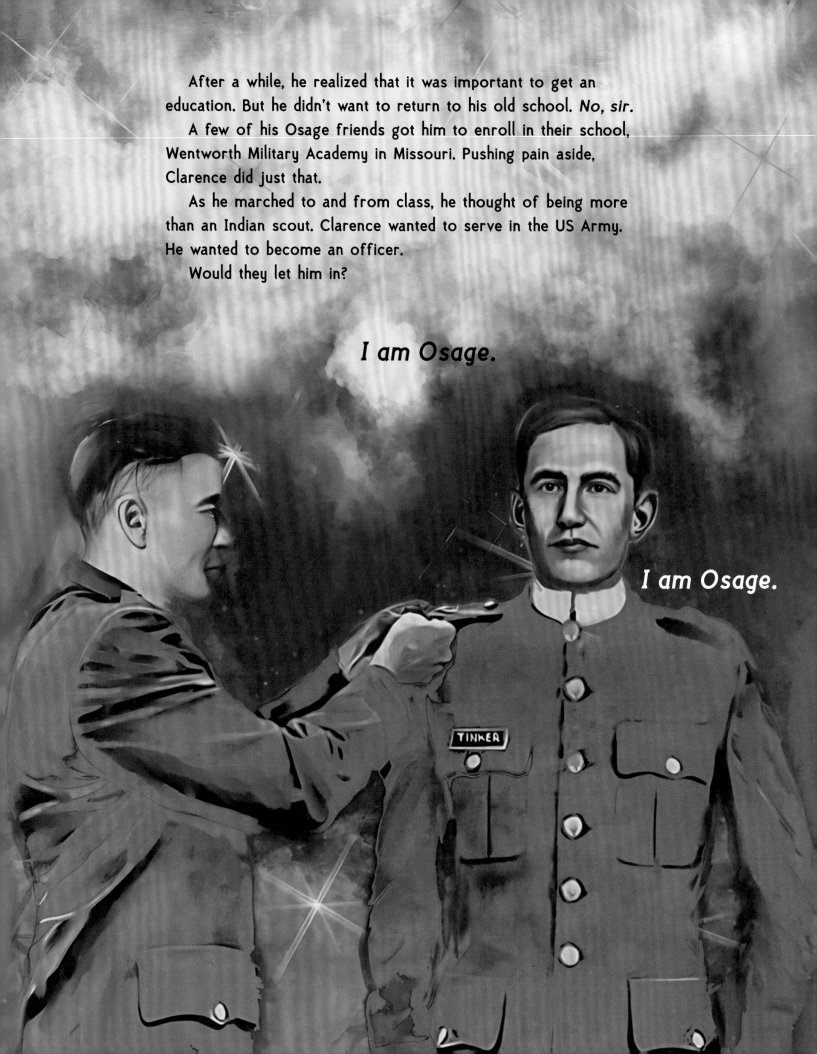

His dream seemed as far away
as the moon and stars.

Clarence did well in school. And his leadership skills shone brighter than bright. A school leader took notice. He recommended Clarence for the army.

After days and days of doubting, on November 3, 1908, Clarence walked across a stage to become a third lieutenant. Some clapped. Some did not . . . probably because they knew . . .

I am Osage.

I am Osage.

Clarence became accustomed to military life, but he wanted more. He learned that another Osage had joined the Army Air Corps. When Clarence thought of becoming a pilot, a new dream took off.

Clarence went to flight school in California. The thrill of adventure quickened his heart. Every time he climbed into the cockpit, his heart thumped like a big ol' Osage drum.

BRUM-BUM-BRUM-BUM . . .

World War I churned far away in Europe, and Clarence wanted to be part of the air combat. But his commanding officer said no.

Is it because I am Osage?

His daddy and other Osages met with the secretary of war Newton D. Baker in Washington, DC. George "Ed" Tinker asked that Clarence be allowed to serve his country where the battle raged.

The next day, Baker told Mr. Tinker that Clarence was one of their finest training officers and too valuable to let go.

All that flattery made Clarence work even harder toward his goal. Clarence got a job teaching ROTC, or Reserve Officers' Training Corps, at Riverside High School in California.

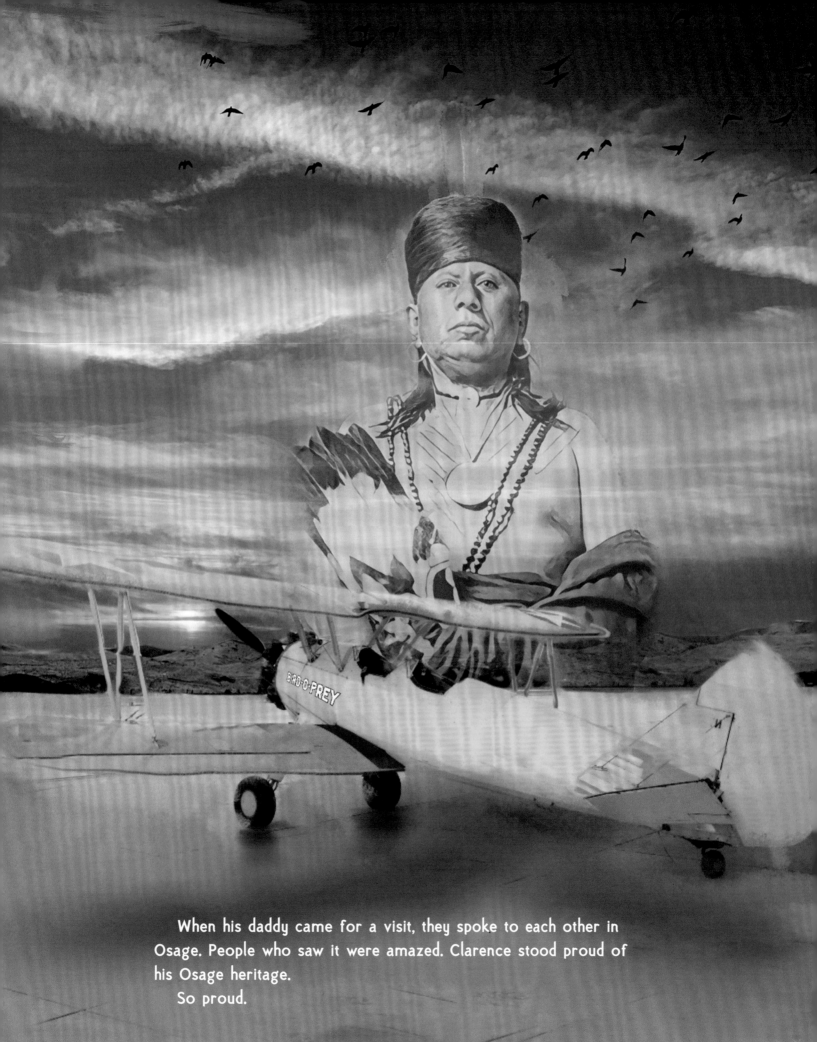

When his daddy came for a visit, they spoke to each other in Osage. People who saw it were amazed. Clarence stood proud of his Osage heritage.
So proud.

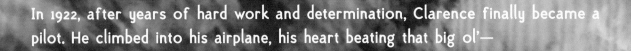

In 1922, after years of hard work and determination, Clarence finally became a
pilot. He climbed into his airplane, his heart beating that big ol'—

BRUM–BUM–BRUM–BUM . . .

He had accomplished his dream. But things still weren't easy.
A dirty look. A sideways glance. A cold shoulder.
But *nothing* discouraged Clarence. He remained strong. He did.

I am Osage.

I am Osage.

In London, he practiced takeoffs and landings with navy commander
Robert A. Burg. The commander asked Clarence to do one more.
All righty, then. Yes, sir!

That time, the engine died as the plane climbed. Clarence wiped his brow
as he kept thinking about what to do. He scanned the patchwork land below,
searching and searching for safe ground.

He clipped trees as he landed. Dizzy, Clarence staggered from the plane.
Oh no! That's when he remembered the commander still in the cockpit.

And he ran back to save him!
Clarence received the Soldier's Medal for his heroism.

Clarence's bravery marched on. In 1924, he was stationed in Missouri. He took off from Richards Field in a small airplane. But during takeoff, the plane's landing gear went all haywire. The officers on the ground radioed him to try to land in the Swope Park lagoon.

Clarence glided the plane near the surface and plunged into the icy-cold water. *Brrr!* He unbuckled his seat belt and swam to the surface . . . where he took a deep breath. *Whew!*

An ambulance raced him back to the airfield lickety-split. But he felt just fine. *Thank you very much, y'all.* He changed clothes and took off again in another airplane!
He wanted to show his men courage.

I am Osage.

I am Osage.

Always a kindhearted gentleman, he treated his men with great respect. He liked them to know how much he cared. He knew every one of their names. When he couldn't remember, he would ask and then want to know more about them.

"What are your duties?"

"How do you like your job?"

"Tell me about your family."

Clarence called them his kids, and they grew to respect him.
His flying and leadership skills amazed his own leaders. He quickly rose
in rank and commanded many bomber units in the 1930s.

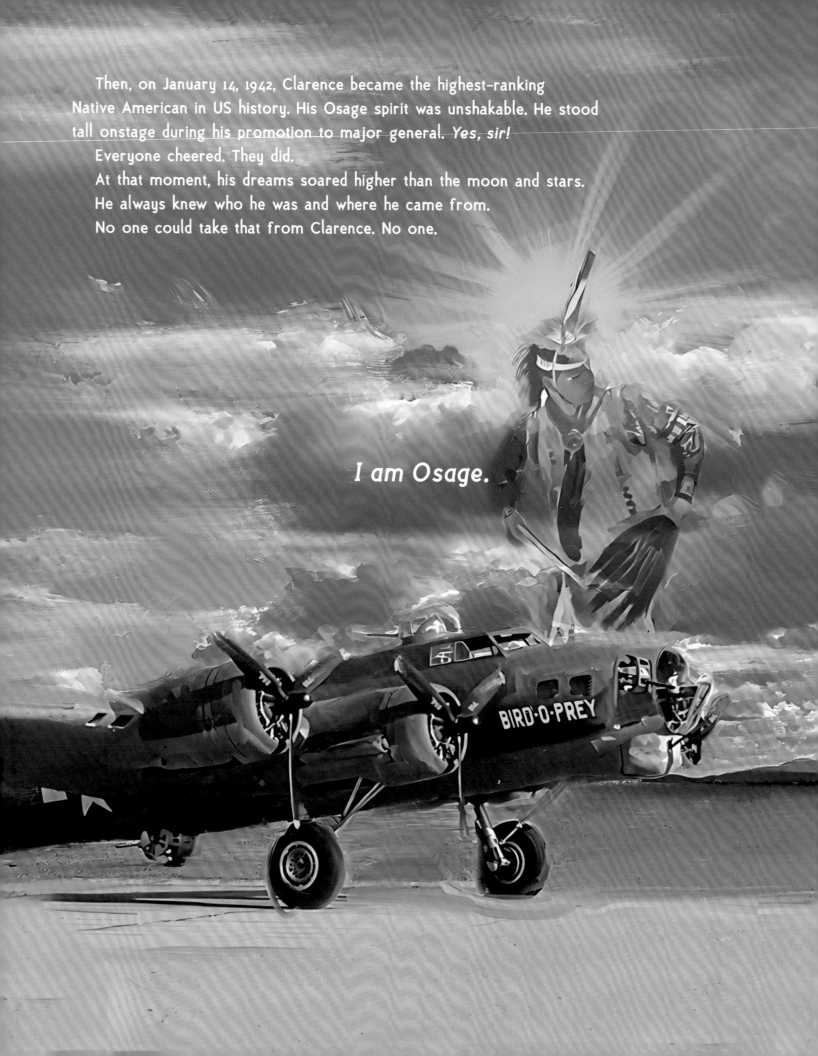

Then, on January 14, 1942, Clarence became the highest-ranking Native American in US history. His Osage spirit was unshakable. He stood tall onstage during his promotion to major general. *Yes, sir!*
Everyone cheered. They did.
At that moment, his dreams soared higher than the moon and stars.
He always knew who he was and where he came from.
No one could take that from Clarence. No one.

I am Osage.

BIRD·O·PREY

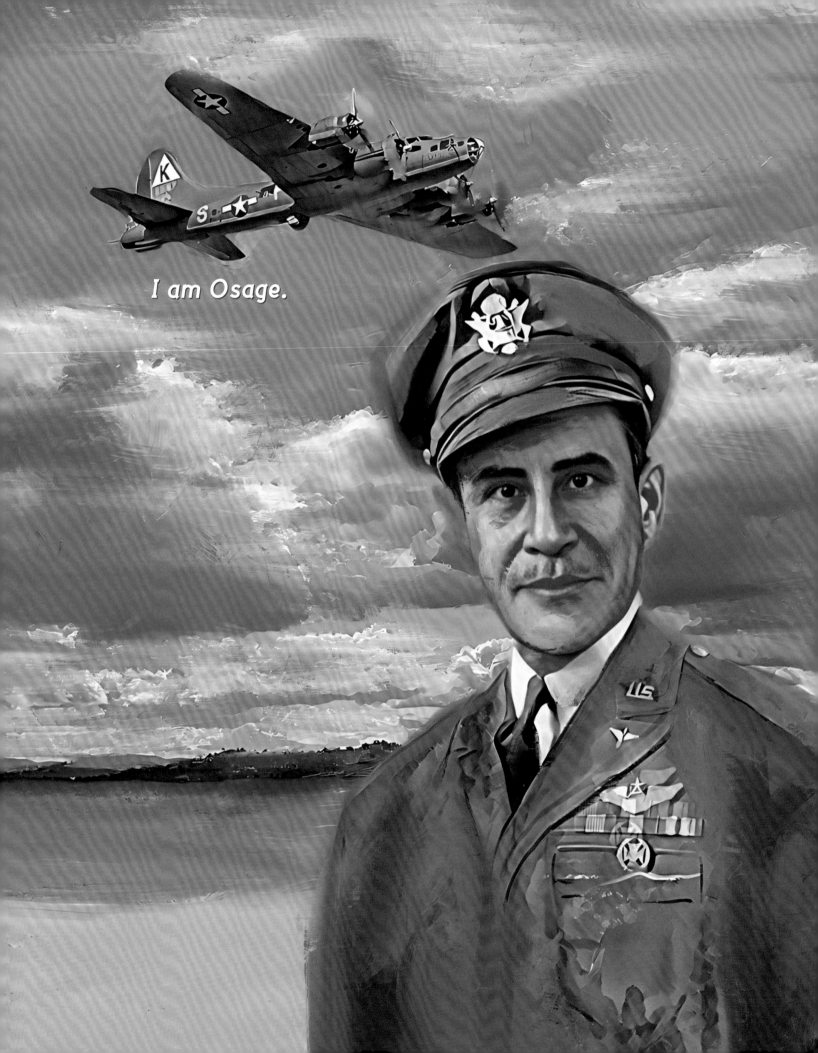

I am Osage.

Clarence died in the Battle of Midway nearly five months later.
And every June since his death, his people sing a drum song they wrote
to honor General Clarence Tinker.

AUTHOR'S NOTE

I'VE ALWAYS BELIEVED that books can bring healing to the reader. Little did I know that writing this book would bring healing to the writer.

From the time I was a young girl, I was often ashamed of my Native American heritage. It made me different. Different from the blond dolls I played with. Different from the white characters I read about in books. Different from my white friends. Different from my white mom, who is rumored to have Native ancestry, but perhaps shame destroyed those records. I wanted to blend in and be just like them.

The shame I'd felt was passed down from my ancestors, who had our Wichita culture stripped from them. As children, they were taken from our family and put into Indian boarding schools. They had their hair cut, were forced to wear white people's clothing, and were punished for speaking Wichita. I can trace this back to our family tree, where I see that my great-great-grandfather Kid-Dah-Wates was forced to change his name to a white name. Next to his Indian name is a dash and "Robert Fulton," the name he chose after the man who invented the steamboat. My other great-great-grandparents were forced to change their names, too.

The land in Indian Territory that was promised forever to my tribe and other tribes was taken away by the government. The Wichita reservation that was established in 1872 would not remain ours. In 1900, it was opened up as surplus lands to white settlers.

Before I was born, my great-grandfather Addison Fulton, who voluntarily served in the navy, moved our family from Anadarko, Oklahoma, to Oklahoma City, where he'd thought we'd have a better life. He even got a job at Tinker Air Force Base. But because of their move, even more of our culture was lost and forgotten. My Wichita grandma did move back to Anadarko years later. And I have fond childhood memories of her taking us to Indian City USA, the American Indian Expo parade, and the Wichita Annual Dance. But those are things I didn't tell my friends.

Clarence Tinker was never ashamed of his Native roots. He was taught in Indian boarding schools to never speak his Osage language. Yet he refused to obey and continued to speak it. The more I researched him, the more inspired I became.

In August 2017, after writing a first draft of this book, I did something I had never done before. I took off the invisible shawl of shame that I had been wearing most of my life and literally put on a Native dance shawl. And I danced for the very first time, in our forty-second Wichita Annual Dance. Tears filled my eyes as I danced to the rhythm of the drum with my Wichita brothers and sisters. Never again will I be ashamed of where I come from.

Because of Clarence Tinker, I was finally able to come home.

Visit the author's website for regularly updated links to research sources.

OSAGE AND WICHITA HISTORY

ALTHOUGH THE OSAGE and Wichita had been enemies for hundreds of years, the Osage allowed my Wichita ancestors to hunt on their land during the Civil War because they were facing starvation. The Osage never harmed or insulted them. The kindness of the Osage people touches me to this day. I am thankful to call them friends.

TIMELINE

1820: Osage representatives ask Right Reverend DuBorg, DD, who was visiting Missouri, to send priests to stay with them and teach their children. Eventually, Catholic and Protestant boarding schools are built and paid for by the tribe. This period of separation from families and loss of culture is a painful time for the Osage.

1825: The US government move the Osage people to a reservation in East Central Kansas.

1870: Osages are forced to move south into Indian Territory in current-day Oklahoma.

1872: The US government force the Osage to move again to land they purchased from the Cherokee Nation near Pawhuska, Oklahoma.

May 12, 1879: Native Americans are declared "persons" or human by a US district court case, *Standing Bear v. Crook*.

November 21, 1887: Clarence Tinker is born in Osage Nation on his grandmother's farm south of Elgin, Kansas.

Dates unknown: It's not clear the years Clarence attends Indian boarding school. His education also comes from several missionary schools run by the Sisters of St. John's in Hominy, Oklahoma; the Sisters of St. Francis in Pawhuska, Oklahoma; and, for a short time, the public school in Elgin, Kansas. He also attended Osage Boarding School in Pawhuska, Oklahoma.

1897: Oil is discovered on the Osage reservation.

November 16, 1907: Oklahoma Territory and Indian Territory merge to become Oklahoma, the forty-sixth state.

1912: Clarence teaches the Twenty-Fifth Infantry at Fort George Wright in Spokane, Washington. It is one of two remaining Black regiments established after the Civil War.

He leads the Black enlisted men to Hawaii, where he lives in a tent.

1913: Clarence marries Madeline Doyle. They have three children together.

August 1914: World War I starts in Europe. George Wright, an Osage agent who is assigned by the government to interact with Osage Indians during the war, tries to discourage the Osage from joining the war because they are not US citizens.

1918: Clarence wants to serve in air combat during World War I. His father, Ed, and other members of the Osage tribe meet with the secretary of war, Newton D. Baker. He tells Ed the next day, "Mr. Tinker, your son is one of the finest training officers in the army, and we can't afford to let him go. He is much too valuable in his present capacity."

1924: Native Americans receive US citizenship.

1925: Because each Osage owns oil rights, people judge them to be the richest tribe in the world. But each Osage is assigned a white guardian to manage their money. Many guardians steal money from them. Clarence isn't even allowed to write his own checks.

1940: The Native American population in the United States is just 350,000, yet more than 44,000 Indigenous people, including Native women, serve in World War II.

June 7, 1942: Clarence Tinker dies at the Battle of Midway during World War II. After Clarence's death, he is awarded the Distinguished Service Medal.

January 13, 1948: The base originally known as Midwest Air Depot is officially named Tinker Air Force Base in honor of Clarence Tinker.

A NOTE FROM CYNTHIA LEITICH SMITH, AUTHOR-CURATOR OF HEARTDRUM

Dear Reader,

Who is your hero? Is it General Clarence Tinker or someone like him who endured struggles and kept the faith—someone who fought to defend their homeland? Is your hero an Elder or a family member or a teacher or a storyteller or maybe even someone your age?

To me, you are heroic. You are heroic when you honor your ancestors, when you live up to your promises, when you overcome hardships, and when you take the loving lessons of your culture to heart.

You are a hero when you believe in yourself.

This picture book is published by Heartdrum, a Native-focused imprint of HarperCollins Children's Books, which highlights stories about Native heroes by Indigenous authors and illustrators. I'm pleased to include this book on the list because it's diligently researched, a compelling read, and illustrated with powerful art. More personally, General Tinker reminds me of my Muscogee grandpa. Like the general, my grandfather was an Indian boarding school survivor who served in the military. When my mother was a little girl, he was stationed at Tinker Air Force Base.

Mvto,

Cynthia Leitich Smith

To my great-grandfather, veterans, and active duty members and their families.
So:ti:cʔa (thank you) all for your service.

—K. R.

I'd like to dedicate this to the Native community and to my family, for always supporting my art and encouraging me to share it with the world.

—B. M.

Heartdrum is an imprint of HarperCollins Publishers.

I Am Osage

Text copyright © 2024 by Kim Rogers

Illustrations copyright © 2024 by Bobby Von Martin

All rights reserved. Manufactured in Italy.

No part of this book may be used or reproduced in any manner whatsoever without written permission except in the case of brief quotations embodied in critical articles and reviews.

For information address HarperCollins Children's Books, a division of HarperCollins Publishers, 195 Broadway, New York, NY 10007.

www.harpercollinschildrens.com • Library of Congress Control Number: 2021057340

ISBN 978-0-06-308116-1 • The artist used acrylic paint assembled digitally to create the illustrations for this book.

23 24 25 26 27 RTLO 10 9 8 7 6 5 4 3 2 1

First Edition

In 2014, We Need Diverse Books (WNDB) began as a simple hashtag on Twitter. The social media campaign soon grew into a 501(c)(3) nonprofit with a team that spans the globe. WNDB is supported by a network of writers, illustrators, agents, editors, teachers, librarians, and book lovers, all united under the same goal—to create a world where every child can see themselves in the pages of a book. You can learn more about WNDB programs at www.diversebooks.org.